IDENTIFIED FLYING OBJECTS

PREVIOUS BOOKS BY MICHAEL BARTHOLOMEW-BIGGS

Poetry

Tell it Like it Might Be, Smokestack Books, 2008

Tradesman's Exit, Shoestring Press, 2010

Fred & Blossom, Shoestring Press, 2013

Pictures from a Postponed Exhibition (with artwork by David Walsh),
Lapwing Publications, 2014

Poems in the Case, Shoestring Press, 2018

IDENTIFIED FLYING

OBJECTS

MICHAEL BARTHOLOMEW-BIGGS

Printed by imprintdigital
Upton Pyne, Exeter
digital.imprint.co.uk

Typesetting and cover design by The Book Typesetters
hello@thebooktypesetters.com
07422 598 168
thebooktypesetters.com

Published by Shoestring Press
19 Devonshire Avenue, Beeston, Nottingham, NG9 1BS
(0115) 925 1827
shoestringpress.co.uk

First published 2024
© Copyright: Michael Bartholomew-Biggs

The moral right of the author has been asserted.

ISBN 978-1-915553-47-8

ACKNOWLEDGEMENTS

Some of these poems (or early versions of them) have previously appeared in the following magazines and books: *Acumen; Clear Poetry; Envoi; Fenland Poetry Journal; Frogmore Papers; The High Window, The Hippocrates Book of the Heart* (Hippocrates Press 2017), *Ink, Sweat & Tears; morphrog; New Welsh Review; Orbis; Penniless Press; Poems for Jeremy Corbyn* (Shoestring Press 2016); *Poems in the Case* (Shoestring Press 2018); *Poetry and All That Jazz; Poetry Salzburg Review; South Bank Poetry; The SHOp; The Spectator* and *Wild Court.* I am grateful to the relevant publishers and editors for their interest in the work.

I am grateful to all those who have commented on poems from this collection, in workshops and elsewhere, during the lengthy period of its composition. In particular I want to extend special thanks to Murray Bodo, Norbert Hirschhorn, Nancy Mattson and Katherine Venn.

CONTENTS

FOREWORD

The poems in this collection can all be seen as responses to quotations from the Old Testament Book of Ezekiel. This does not mean that they paraphrase Ezekiel's message or offer a commentary on it; and none of the voices should be thought of as belonging to the prophet. Some of the poems do place an Ezekiel-like (or Ezekiel-lite!) speaker into a present-day setting; but others simply offer a, possibly tangential, twenty-first century reaction to an idea or image in the Biblical text. Ezekiel might recognise – even endorse – the sentiments of a few of the poems; but many of them would probably puzzle him or even arouse his disapproval.

During the 6th century BC the people of Israel suffered military defeats at the hands of the Babylonians and many of them were subsequently taken as captives to Babylon. The Book of Ezekiel sets out to explain the spiritual reasons behind this national disaster. Ezekiel himself was among the earliest groups to be exiled and he had to prepare his companions for the even worse news that Jerusalem itself would soon be captured and yet more of their countrymen deported. While Ezekiel regarded defeat and captivity as a deserved consequence of national failure to keep God's commandments, he did also offer the people hope of an eventual restoration to their homeland. Some commentators suggest that these sections of the book prefigure the message of forgiveness and renewal that characterises the Christian gospels.

Whatever one believes about its theological content, the Book of Ezekiel does contain some remarkable passages – most notably the prophet's vision of a mysterious but quite precisely described vessel which brings the likeness of God's glory from heaven down to earth. (This account includes the first use of the well-known phrase "wheels within wheels".) Ezekiel also makes what is surely the first proposal for a heart transplant; and one of his visions of a better future features an almost cinematic image of a valley littered with dry bones which reassemble themselves before gaining sinews, flesh and skin to become living bodies. More down-to-earth (and still relevant today) are the stern and imaginative rebukes he delivers to corrupt and abusive rulers and his exasperated likening of human behaviour to that of ill-natured sheep led by incompetent and irresponsible shepherds.

Ezekiel sometimes used striking public performances to enhance his challenging messages. He acted out the siege of Jerusalem while lying down in the public square for many weeks. On other occasions he illustrated the scattering of his people by tossing his own shaven hair into the wind and burrowed through an earth wall to show how the nation's leaders would try to escape the fate that awaited their fellow citizens.

The idea of basing a poem sequence on the Book of Ezekiel came to me some years ago when I was convalescing after a road accident which had left me with a broken leg. (Direct reference to this event and its consequences is made in the curtain-raising 'Physiotherapy' poems as well as in the main sequence.) The first poems to be written were some of the more political ones which re-directed Ezekiel's warnings about Jerusalem toward a city bearing some resemblance to London ('Street Theatre', 'Free Running', 'Charisma of a False Prophet'). The later inclusion of more personal (and even frivolous) material reflected a change in my "relationship" with Ezekiel. While I admired his eloquence against injustice and corruption and his insistence that bad situations could be mended and renewed, I also had to deal with (or ignore) his more punitive, dogmatic and nationalistic attitudes. Since our lives are two and half thousand years apart, it is quite possible that Ezekiel's view of my own preconceptions could include a Hebrew equivalent of the word "woke". But even so – and even if I have casually and anachronistically appropriated his work for my own purposes – I hope that he and I might still find some common ground among the poems which follow.

Bible quotations come from the (public domain) World English Bible.

PHYSIOTHERAPY PART 1 (THEORY)

Seen from a window, halfway up the hillside,
round hedges cushioning the valley's vee
resemble parallel upholstered bars.

They support stray thoughts of damaged limbs
re-learning joined-up steps between soft lines –
like spelling out a sentence with blunt crayon.

Then imagination skips ahead
and writes a gymnast's alphabet of X
and Y inverted, upright bold-faced I.

He is neither amputee nor athlete
so today he saunters down the lane
between its banks of brambles and small blooms

and rubs against a rarely flowering grace
that, while it lasts, will ask a given moment
for nothing more or less than what it brings.

PHYSIOTHERAPY PART 2 (PRACTICE)

That first part could be seen as tempting fate.
Years later, when a badly broken femur
put him in a wheelchair then on crutches,

he was exiled from all public spaces
reached by steps and quite invisible
on pavements till he got in someone's way.

A van had run him over and without
Ezekiel to tell him he deserved it
and to promise rehabilitation

he took it as bad luck. To compensate
he exercised and soon he quite enjoyed
the crutch-and-handrail trick for climbing stairs.

And even now when walking between tables
he will take his weight on arms and shoulders
and leave his legs free-swinging like a child.

INTERNAL EXILE

Two ways to learn you don't belong in Babylon.

The first, most obvious: somebody drags you there
with all your neighbours, puts you on a reservation
where there's shade enough and water. You're exhibits
though the fact you've been collected matters more
than who you are. Spectators sometimes watch and prod you
for amusement but your repertoire of zoo songs
has been lost along with all your other playthings
thrown among the bushes. Trees above your head
ooze misery like honeydew. It sticks to you.
Dust sticks to it. In grubby secrecy you plot
appalling retribution for your kidnappers.

The second starts at home: you realise your neighbours
are establishing a Babylon around you,
disciplining grass you left un-mown last year.
They're planting borders in (they say) the proper way
replacing new varieties of fruiting bush
with hedges and a maze that only they can thread.
You learn you never knew them. Nor do they know you.
They talk of building walls with towers, flagpoles, flags
above an avenue of statues: you suggest
the ground won't bear the weight. They try to drown you out
by bellowing, dead-eyed, an old song of denial.

I was among the captives by the river Chebar... in the land of the Babylonians
Ezekiel 1:1

Ezekiel makes clear that he identifies with his exiled compatriots in Babylon. The
poem imagines other kinds of banishment or alienation and draws on Psalm 137,
"By the waters of Babylon", an exiles' lament (sometimes attributed to the
prophet Jeremiah) which has often been borrowed for popular songs in our own
time.

IDENTIFIED FLYING OBJECTS

Sceptics guess that magic mushrooms helped
to open Heaven – or perception's doors –
in Babylon and show the awed and shocked
Ezekiel some version of
the gyroscope and helicopter
in advance of L. da Vinci.

Ezekiel did not make sketches. He left
words instead of blueprints. Hence his engines,
while attracting less mechanical
analysis than Leonardo's,
leave a lot more room for extra
terrestrial imaginings.

Some fantasists insist that aliens
can scrawl art deco doodles in our fields
and navigate the planet via ley lines.
Others say time-travellers
could show Ezekiel a future
three millennia ahead.

Perhaps he caught a glimpse of locust-gunships
stuttering across Iraqi deserts,
stop-start – like the freeze-frame hovering
of hummingbirds he'd never known –
and bringing down much cruder forms
of shock and awe on Babylon.

> *[T]he heavens were opened, and I saw visions of God… Out of its centre came the likeness of four living creatures. … There was one wheel on the earth beside the living creatures … Their appearance and their work was as it were a wheel within a wheel. … When the living creatures were lifted up from the earth, the wheels were lifted up.*
> **Ezekiel 1:1–19**

Some explain Ezekiel's vision as a clairvoyant's (or time-traveller's) preview of modern – perhaps military – technology. Josef Blumrich (*The Spaceships of Ezekiel* 1974) claims it describes a genuine extraterrestrial encounter of the kind reported in literature dedicated to phenomena like UFOs, ley lines and crop circles.

PUSHED AROUND IN STEPNEY GREEN

Narrow pavements and abrupt unfriendly kerbs
test your novice wheelchair-steering skills
and my tolerance for jolts. A turning
tips us into Sidney Street which suddenly
reminds me of a standoff featuring police
and stranded anarchists from Latvia.
At the siege of Sidney Street young Winston Churchill
showed up to be present for the showdown
but was upstaged by one agitator's absence.
Peter Pjatkov – dubbed "The Painter" – wasn't
ever traced, alive or dead, and might have been
a nihilist who never did exist.

I tell you this tall tale until we reach a park
that should be unremarkable. Today –
and *pace* Joni Mitchell – it's a shrubby unpaved
paradise among the East End's grubby flagstones.
It feels welcome as that tiny gravel square
in Venice where we saw small children play
on stones and *earth* (we'd had enough for one weekend
of bloody water and those damned canals).
In Stepney Green the swings and slides are overlooked
by whitewashed maisonettes. The dogs and toddlers
living there enjoy small freedoms among borders
where the bushes breathe out herbal remedies.

You turn the wheelchair round and point me back
toward the ward where views are sliced at rooftop height
by rows of small-paned windows that won't open.
There I'll be well-meaningly besieged
by nurses (some of whom may come from Latvia)
while orderlies keep anarchy at bay.

When the living creatures went the wheels went beside them. **Ezekiel 1:19**

For an account of the 1911 Siege of Sidney Street see *en.wikipedia.org/wiki/ Siege_of_Sidney_Street*

MAIDEN SPEECH

This new arrival (where's he from again?) has swallowed more
than any other member of this House can chew.
Which he'll regurgitate until they're edgy on their padded seats
and wriggle to distract themselves and distance what he says
from how it's said.

        They may admit his knack with rhetoric but mock
his ignorance of how the world must work. He'll have no truck
with what he calls the politics of scorpions
and economics founded on a currency of thorns.

Opponents from all sides make speeches but they can't obscure
his questions – though they try. They blame his ambiguity.
Each side can understand the other. One side pretends it can't.

This frowning man lets bitter words go tumbling from his tongue
into their ears – to sabotage their balance, make them gag
and squirm like scorpions who'll sting themselves to death.

> *Don't be afraid of their words, nor be dismayed at their looks, though they are a
> rebellious house. You shall speak my words to them, whether they will hear, or whether
> they will refuse.* **Ezekiel 2:6–7**

The terms of Ezekiel's call to confront his nation and its leaders can also apply to
anyone aspiring to cut through the cant of an entrenched ruling group.

BITTER ALMONDS

He didn't know they grew in England – let alone
beside the footpath he was treading. He was eight.
He'd seen them in the shops but with their light brown shells
exposed and not disguised in smooth green padded jerkins,
which, misleadingly, looked softer than they felt –
like kittens' velvet paws concealing knuckle bones.

So he'd not have known what lay beneath that tree
beside the path they'd never gone along before
(the one that started near the churchyard where dead soldiers
from the barracks had been buried). He would not
have known, that is, if others hadn't been there first
who'd stepped on shells and split them. Possibly his mother

wanted to distract him from the other questions
he kept asking; so she stooped and picked one up
but wouldn't let him taste what might be poisonous.
She said they'd better take some home to show his father
who was trusted to know everything that mattered
even though a lot was on his mind just then

and that was why the two of them alone were walking
through this wood round which the main road made a dog-leg
(*why not cat?* he wondered). They went back the long way,
staying out till they were sure the visitor
at home had gone. His mother didn't need to know
what happened or what attitudes had ripened there

so long as neither of them stepped on pavement cracks
or trampled fallen fruit. His father, waiting for them
at the gate, ignored their clutch of suspect nuts
and talked toward his mother awkwardly, as if
on tiptoe, placing words precisely as a cat's paws
finding gaps between their household ornaments.

and I went in bitterness, ... and I sat there overwhelmed **Ezekiel 3:14,15**

STREET THEATRE

He wonders why his precious flesh remains
unbruised beside the gutters of Barbican
where he's laid himself down and kept
extended silence. He remembers sighing
when he acquiesced to wearing shackles
as a wider warning of impending
penalties.

                         Black axioms
are hidden in the pockets of dark suits
on money men who must step round him.
As they do, far more of them
ignore him than will meet his eyes
or scan his dumb-show doomsday tokens.

Amid the mud he is meticulous
to promise no more than he knows
and threaten nothing less. No softening
of his position is permitted
to trip up passers-by and overturn
their bland indifference to sewage stink
and wet corruption clinging to their ankles.

He marvels that his holy bones
still hold together in his fragile carcase.

> *[T]ake a tile, and lay it before yourself, and portray on it a city, even Jerusalem. Lay siege against it … Moreover lie on your left side and lay the iniquity of the house of Israel on it.* **Ezekiel 4:1 & 4**

> Ezekiel is told to enact the siege and fall of a city whose inhabitants are to blame for its impending destruction.

IN THE FITTING ROOM

The mirror switches *left* and *right* without transposing
top and *bottom* – same as always; but today
you note this perpendicular discrepancy
while recognizing it is not the only one.
A flat-earth model offers horizontal freedoms –
you can wander *north* to *south* or *east* from *west* –
yet vertical's another story. Two more stories
more precisely: *down* can fly away with you
till free fall reaches terminal velocity;
but efforts to rise *up* won't be a great success.

You aren't too much distressed that you can't levitate
but frequently resent those day to day restraints
imposed in terms of longitude and latitude:
keep left; no entry; one way only; stay in lane.
You reckon limits on a change of altitude
are inescapable and no more worth protesting
than the looking-glass's inconsistency.
The laws of optics and of gravity arise
elsewhere. (You'd use a capital and write Elsewhere
if you'd the kind of mind inclined to reverence.)

You wonder now what analogue of magnetism
moves your moral compass. Being *right* or *wrong*
might be about alignment with some field of force
whose source (big S or small) is far away. If so
you'll be compliant since complaints are futile
as expletives flung by someone falling from a ladder.
But you'll fight if self-appointed censors try to
drag you down some straight and narrow alleyway
they once were forced along themselves by other parties
claiming upper-case Authority to do so.

Behold, I put ropes on you, and you shall not turn yourself from one side to the other
Ezekiel 4:8

11

CAUTION TO THE WINDS

In the end so much depends upon the madmen.
Unconcerned with how their actions might be judged
they'll ride upon their wrath without a single doubt.
It's fear of being singled out for disapproval
that de-motivates accomplishers of nothing
more than signing earnest letters and petitions.

Frustration oozes out in public like the vapour
round a safety valve. It's in that *sotto voce*
tuneless whistle coming from the seat behind you,
as the occupant drums fingers on the window.
Travellers whose carry-on is everlasting
rage know what to break in an emergency.

Unrest erupting randomly is hard to stop
and tests the limits of the force of law and order.
When policemen waste their time and try to read
the minds of holy fools they have to leave unwatched
those shrewder schemers who slip in behind the chaos
daubing slogans while they dream of drafting laws.

> *You, son of man, take a sharp sword. … as a barber's razor … to pass over your head*
> *and over your beard. [W]eigh and divide the hair. A third you shall burn… take a*
> *third and strike with the sword … one third you shall scatter to the wind*
> **Ezekiel 5:1,2**

Evidently Ezekiel was exceptionally unselfconscious about making a spectacle of
himself.

MILD ZEALOT

You imagined you would go
among them as a supper-guest
and at the meal wax eloquent
by candlelight reflected from their saffron table cloth.

You imagined shadowed faces
turned toward you – faces less
important than philosophies,
elaborate with axioms you'd have to undermine.

And you would undermine them kindly,
while they worked out for themselves
how many of their old conclusions
could still stand on those few axioms you let them keep.

You intended to be patient
with their struggles as you stripped them
of their well-worn certainties
then once undressed they could put on your ready-made designs.

Your bearded host would reach across
an empty but still fragrant dish
to take your hands in gratitude ....

It happened not as you'd imagined but in unkempt rooms.
They lacked the diffidence you'd scripted,
spoke of sickness, tax and rumour,
troubled neither by their errors
nor your arguments and morbid need for confrontation.

They will know that I have spoken in my zeal **Ezekiel 5:13**

CAGLIOSTRO STREET

Cagliostro Street does not exist
on maps but in a novel's pages
and the minds of readers
like my father. Here's his copy (spoiler:
Dr Grimaud's killer is
the man who wasn't there).

Cagliostro Street does not exist
but poses as a *cul de sac*
close to Russell Square
and from its entrance witnesses observe
a man shot dead: the gunman's hand
is nowhere near the gun.

Cagliostro Street – should it exist –
must run from Guilford Place behind
the children's hospital
from where the dying victim's anxious daughter
notices the lights go on
in an artist's love nest.

    *

Is there such a street? I went to search
but drew a blank and sketched this poem
in a local café.
There a well-known intellectual –
unkempt and loud – was holding forth
across a dish of pasta.

Dr Grimaud too liked lecturing
to friends assembled round his table.
This philosopher
was castigating British diplomats
who'd overlooked atrocities
committed by the wealthy

president of Somewherestan whose syntax
treats the verb *to disappear*
as being transitive.
You could say that the victim disappeared
the perpetrator of the crime
on Cagliostro Street.

       *

Cagliostro Street does not exist
but it's where I'll find my father
if I lose myself,
as he could, in fantastic narratives
of sealed-room crimes and even more
improbable events.

> *the land is full of bloody crimes, and the city is full of violence.* **Ezekiel 7:23**

The 1936 mystery novel *The Hollow Man* by John Dickson Carr features murders which occur in "impossible" situations.

FREE RUNNING

A runner's coming in a linen loin cloth,
a tight-corked inkwell swinging from his belt.
His feet in sandals patter over paving
slabs along triumphal avenues
or skid on straw and faeces in dark alleys.

His stylus doubles as a baton, passed
between the dozens like him, checking scores
of zig-zag streets – and getting close. Yet mostly
he's ignored: he's no Olympic torch-man,
cheered on through a smug metropolis.

He tells us grieving's what we have to do
to gain exemption from whatever vengeance
is predicted for our city's misdeeds.
Better shed real tears: we can't assume
self-righteous grumbling gets us any marks.

> *he called to the man clothed in linen, who had the writer's inkhorn by his side...*
> *"Go through the middle of the city, ..., and set a mark on the foreheads of the men*
> *that sigh and that cry over all the abominations that are done within it."*
> **Ezekiel 9:3–4**

Ezekiel's picture calls to mind the 2012 London Olympics which began as a self-congratulatory affair that some of us – quite wrongly – predicted would be an embarrassing failure.

VISITING MY PAST ON GOOGLE MAPS™

The cursor scrolls across a bird's-eye view
with labels but no contour-lines to show
how suddenly my level Middlesex
has bulged into this unexpected hill
   on which I'm running, cold and wet,
   a little way ahead of Christmas 1960.

   This is not the race, simply a practice run
   through dusk that's earlier and gloomier
   than usual under grubby rainclouds.
   When the actual race occurs I won't be winning
   but I'd rather be an also-ran, short-winded
   on the final climb toward the tape,
   than left behind at school among the sick-notes
   and the hopelessly unfit.

   This is not the race, so I can stop for breath
   and take in all that's sprawled below me:
   muddy meadows, held in check by hedges,
   sloping down to towpath and canal;
   a pair of local trains criss-crossing
   silently like strings of fairy lights;
   threaded amber beads of streetlamps
   marking rows of huddled houses much like mine;
   the distant glassworks, like a model of itself,
   radiates a reddish glow
   as homely as a fire for roasting chestnuts.

I'm scanning that terrain again, now digitised,
to check my memory, correcting distances.
Paths I trudged are overgrown: I search for them
with software tools unheard-of
   when with only eyes and intuition
   I am out-of-body hovering
   above the diorama I inhabit;

and though my limbs are shivering
and wholly present on this dismal hillside
they are also back at home
remembering the chill they're feeling now
while I'm already running a hot bath
and cramming in a slab of bread and jam
as I rehearse my Christmas expectations.

It's a moment when I find awareness
needn't stay confined to any single anywhere.
This insight – even while I'm getting it – insists
it will be – and deserves to be – remembered
as indeed it is. Right now, as I create
a similar escape from tedium
imagining myself both *here* and *there*
and hoping *now* and *then* can co-exist.

Nostalgia flourishes like weeds and shrubs
in lockdown on an undistinguished hillside
when there's too much unclaimed space-time handy.

In this poem, the actions of the "urban runner" from Ezekiel 9:3 are followed by personal recollections of a twentieth-century suburban one.

IS ANYBODY THERE?

Science twists a fairy tale
into a systematic quest
for Goldilocks in Ursa Major
and/or Minor to discover
who's been sitting/eating/ sleeping
in a *just right* orbit – one
that's *not too hot and not too cold –*
where life has had a sporting chance
of being *as we know it, Jim.*

Astronomers have spotted eight
such planets so far – so far off
they have no clue who's lurking out there:
could be Klingons, could be Clangers.

Strange new worlds may hold fresh creatures
we would not have dreamt of once
upon a time; but even if
our planet ceased to be unique
we'd want to be *by no means least*
and think the stars will always shine
upon us with uncommon favour.
(Some astrologers will cite
the special case of Bethlehem.)

> *This is the living creature that I saw ... and I knew that they were cherubim....
> The likeness of the hands of a man was under their wings.* **Ezekiel 10:20–21**

Ezekiel gives two descriptions of a mysterious heavenly vehicle and its occupants.
Belief in the existence of human – or at least humanoid – creatures elsewhere in
the universe is, however, not confined to religious mystics and science-fiction
enthusiasts. Astronomers search for potentially life-supporting planets orbiting in
so-called "Goldilocks zones" around a central star. This poem borrows from Gene
Roddenberry (author of *Star Trek*), Oliver Postgate (creator of the BBC Children's
series *Clangers*) and the prophet Micah

URBAN CONCEALMENT

The city is reticent about its past.
The not-so-well-remembered layers:
fallen walls, worn floors,
smashed grave- and paving-stones,
stay folded like a gambler's cards –
private even as the lifelines
on the gambler's hand.

The present fills in spaces
between pencil strokes:
the horizontal lintels over doorways;
verticals of lightning rods
and empty flagpoles.

Criss-cross window grills
are shadow-doubled
onto kitchen whitewash;
banister diagonals
smooth the saw-tooth of a staircase
to a long descending slide.

Though the city does not speak
its surfaces are open
to arbitrary messages.

Among graffiti tags,
as meaningless as punctuation
in a rubbed-out sentence,
the cemetery wall
is carrying a love note
to the local football team

and by a dried-up fountain
sprayed black paint announces
*You can't stop the sun
with a policeman's gun.*

The city is reticent about its past.
Too-many-to-remember layers
of betrayals, failed alliances
and deals unrealised are locked
in legal boxes and confessionals –
or else forgotten utterly
like an unmarked grave.

these are the men who devise iniquity, and who give wicked counsel in this city; who say, 'The time is not near to build houses. This is the cauldron, and we are the meat.'
Ezekiel 11:2–3

This poem also draws on *"Le città invisibili"* by Italo Calvino.

LUMB BANK TO LONDON WITH A TRAVELLING COMPANION

I was in my mid-life crisis at the time
with plenty to forget.
Bad poet, I was heading with a passenger
down a motorway I'd travelled up alone
a week before to get to Yorkshire
where I might learn to be a better one.

She'd thrown away her unused ticket home
and I'd renounced my former destination.
We abandoned bowls of untouched fruit
and said goodbye
to everybody we'd sat down to breakfast with.

Driving south – but often turning east or west –
we hurtled past grey, fabled and forbidding cities
talking over last week's poetry tutorials
and the seminars on Blaise Cendrars.
I was feeling younger with each mile.

Tell me, are we nearly there?
If she'd said that, could I take it as a joke?
Or a sign she now regretted riding side by side
while damaging our smiles with Trebor mints?
Or was it simply she was still a stranger in my country?

Near Sheffield I could speak with little authenticity
of steel cold-rolled in Attercliffe and Tinsley;
Nottingham, I said, meant dainty lace; but Leicester
was still keeping Richard Crookback's secret
over-staying underneath a car park.

Tell me, are we nearly there?
Bad navigator, I could hardly tell her,
if she'd asked, how far we'd yet to go
until we'd synchronised our histories
and our expectations.

As we brushed suburban petticoats
of bleak, prosaic Milton Keynes
she fell asleep and in the quiet of her breathing
I remembered we were nearly where
a village leans against a long straight street
and shops sell handlebars and saddle soap.
I stopped to close an empty house I'd left unlocked.

When we were on wheels again
our wheels were on the road again to London.
Would we be always on that road to London?

Awake once more, she made me follow London buses
till we reached a street beside a strip of water
lined with houseboats. Smells of coal smoke
curled through iron railings. Unpretentious vessels
held out narrow gangplanks.
She told me we were nearly there
but that was not the there she'd brought us to.

Across the road were metal steps descending to a basement.
So we were not about to float away downstream
on board a cliché
neither near nor far from anywhere.

We were, in point of fact, right at the point
of disembarking from the nondescript.
Perhaps entirely. And perhaps forever.
This bad poem testifies that any credit
must belong to her.
All the infelicities are mine.

> *I will be to them a sanctuary for a little while in the countries where they have come.*
> **Ezekiel 11:16**

> Ezekiel's picture of finding a place of safety is here re-imagined after reading *Prose du Transsibérien* by Blaise Cendrars.

FORTHCOMING EVENTS

You've grown accustomed to old pessimists
who get things wrong. That forecast of a leader leaving
by a side way with his famous face concealed
forever was much overstated. He did nicely
in retirement with a pension and the standard knighthood.

You've grown accustomed to old pessimists
like pigeons on a ledge – a nuisance to ignore.
Crumb-scrounging and defeatist flutterings
seem minor irritants; those intermittent squirts
of excrement on windows soon get wiped away.

Now this latest unkempt pessimist
insists that all the former pessimists were right
but premature. They marked the trees that are diseased
or lacking fruit for want of proper pruning: only
now are men with axes really on the way.

> *what is this proverb that you have … saying, 'The days are prolonged, and every vision fails?' I will make this proverb to cease, and they will no more use it*
> **Ezekiel 12:22–23**

Ezekiel has just predicted the nation's leaders will run away and try to save themselves; but he soon encounters the disbelief of sceptics who suggest they've "had about enough of experts".

WINTER ON THE RYE
After a print by Paul Benjamins

And what do hedgerows hide
as night submerges them?
Fox barks punctuate the dusk. Small rodents
feed on seeded scraps. Whatever's lost,
unwanted by the loser,
pins itself against a bush for burning
when a sunset pinks the middle-distance mist
and far-away geometries of swirling clouds.

Dark is eating up old footpaths.
Newer muddy tracks lead back
to where we've been before
from unremembered angles
through dimensions of the common-
place we always were too occupied
with better things to mention.

your prophets have been like foxes in the waste places. **Ezekiel 13:4**

IMAGE CONSULTANT

He rolls his eyes whenever managers declare
We'll always circulate full details
about any new procedure we propose
so staff can have their say.
If they approve then we will recommend
that everyone adopt it right away;
but if they're not so keen
we'll tell them it's compulsory next week.

He understands both conjurers and cardsharps,
knows the showman and the charlatan
take pride in skilful misdirection.
But tricksters who succeed in politics
believe they can dispense with sleight of hand
and telegraph what's coming next.
When they reveal the card they've crudely palmed
a compère madly calls for loud applause.
The doltish crowd is eager to oblige.

He sighs while each new Minister of Self-Protection
promises *If policies don't work*
I'll launch a rigorous Enquiry
with an e in upper case and Chaired
by Someone of the Proper Sort.
He'll sift the facts and find the few that show me
in good light; or, failing that, adjourn
until my name no longer rhymes with blame.

> *these men have taken their idols into their heart,.... Should I be inquired of at all by them?* **Ezekiel 14:3**

Ezekiel complains of those who go through the motions of seeking advice when their prejudices prevent them from accepting an answer.

CONFUSING THE MESSAGE

If you're opposed to all the outcomes
don't seek guidance. And ignore it
when God knows the questions you don't
ask and answers anyway.

A maiden may become a mother.
Sometimes little boys are born
without a father who decides
the proper kind of proper name.

So many little boys are born
and few will thrive while more go short.
It's either fruit and cream or curds
and honey gathered wild through stings.

While few will thrive and more go short
most reach an age when they aspire
to be grownup – to know what's best
and not be told *you must* or *don't*.

You've reached that age: at least aspire
to make a fist of each fresh choice.
You may try hard to seem in charge
but still be bending with events.

To make a fist suggests a choice
to recognize an enemy
and start a fight. You hope your friends
will rally round – but you'd be wise

to recognize some enemies
go soft like honey in the sun
while allies quickly melt away
if you serve them only curds.

If you despise the other party
don't sign treaties. Winning friends
beats cutting deals for keeping people
well and truly on your side.

This poem is also based on Ezekiel 14:3 but also borrows extensively from
Isaiah 7.

AT THE WELL

And then he asked me for drink.
Just like that: would you believe it?
I had to show I'd not put up with being put upon:
remember who you are, I said, and what I am,
and don't play games with me.

He took it in his stride.
I'm not exactly who you think I am, he said.
At least, I am that too; but that's not all I am.
If you could see beyond my face and accent you'd soon know
I'm someone who's got something that you need.

Well, that's a sort of talk I've heard a dozen times before;
though, to be fair, I'm not sure if he meant it quite that way.
But, seeing where we were, I told him
I'd be more impressed if he could meet my need
to not be trudging to and from this well each day.
Had he ever had a go at doing that?
No, I thought he wouldn't have.
(And you'd think our menfolk would have learned
a thing or two concerning pipework
since the occupying army came.)

Then he tried another tack – to see if I was unattached?
Go and get your husband, he says briskly –
as if he'd now got bored with me.
I could have palmed him off of course
and claimed the master of the house was off on business:
no way could he have called my bluff.

Or so I thought.
Turns out the cheeky blighter knew it all the time –
the partners I'd already been through.
And the bloke that's with me now.
(It's not so hard round here to pick up gossip.)

Funny, though, he didn't sneer about my past or present.
That's right, he said, well done, you told the truth.
And then I sort of knew he'd not
been hanging round the neighbours asking questions.
He'd read my thoughts. Or my red face.

I've got your number now, I said.
You're one of those religious blokes
who *know* things, aren't you? Up here from the city
where they do the worship now and tell us
praying on the mountain isn't right and proper any more.
You lot have hijacked all the things our Dads believed.

There's more to it than that, he said.
It's not your place or mine that matters.
In the end it's not so much the *where*
you go to pray, it's more the *how*.
That's something my folks need to learn as much as yours.

Sounds like a teaching job for someone pretty special then, I said.
Someone who can overturn a *status quo*
as *quo* as what we're stuck with now.
A somebody a bit like you, is what I thought –
although I'd swear I never said that part out loud.

That's it. You've got it, he replied.

Samaria and her daughters will return to their former estate **Ezekiel 16:55**

In Ezekiel 16 the prophet itemizes the wrongdoing of Israel and her neighbour
Samaria yet also promises the fortunes of both will one day be restored. Even so,
Samaritans were still looked down on by Jews in New Testament times 500 years
later. The poem is based on the highly unorthodox conversation between Jesus
and a Samaritan woman recorded in John 4:4–42.

TAKING NOTICE

It's been so long since you gave any thought to blue tits.
They might as well have ceased existing
though they seemed like *feathered friends*
when you were small. They'd peck through silver foil
on doorstep bottles for the cream –
in evolutionary terms
a *cul de sac,* it now turns out, since milk has been
homogenised or semi-skimmed.
You don't expect to see a blue tit any more
than dairymen delivering.

Today you spotted movement on a leafless branch:
your eyes could only register
its shape; but buried memory
supplied the blue and yellow vest and jacket.
You're charmed but guiltily surprised
by your surprise at this reminder:
blue tits do still land on squares of urban garden.
You had even missed the fact
that they seemed missing. You'd not missed them
and a voice, insistent as a songbird's warning,
starts to chirp *What else? What else?*

> *it will produce boughs, and bear fruit, and be a good cedar. Birds of every kind will dwell in the shade of its branches.* **Ezekiel 17:23**

These words are part of a lengthy parable and Ezekiel does not comment much on real nature in the world around him. That however is no reason to become inattentive …

FAMILY OCCASION

Hallo Dad, he says, *this is me Mum*
and everybody starts to laugh:

the son, his girlfriend and the mother
eating at an outside table.

The father's only just turned up. He stays
beyond the café's pavement space.

Their chat soon moves to holidays – but whose?
It must be obvious to them

though I can't tell if they are sharing plans,
reports or reminiscences.

The late arrival leaves again
amid much loud, good-natured waving.

Did that opening joke simply imply
one member of a close-knit clan

had been away so long that he might struggle
to remember who they were?

Or was it one more try at dealing with
the rueful mutual recognition

of survivors from a broken marriage
still living in the same small town
since no one can afford to move away?

> *The fathers have eaten sour grapes, and the children's teeth are set on edge*
> **Ezekiel 18:2**

IS THAT *REALLY* HOW TO DO IT?

Transporting half a dozen Dorset men on trumped-up evidence:
the gentry's way of thwarting calls to raise farm workers' pay.
A rich man later builds the six a thatched memorial.

On Derby Day, a reckless suffragette brings down the King's
own horseman
greatly scandalising Middle England's media
which these days lets us glimpse that newsreel like a holy relic.

In the end, descendants, counterparts
and clones of those who used to loathe protesters
learn to criticise (or fail to praise)
such forbears as the merchants and MPs
who mocked Sam Plimsoll's loading safety rules
or treated shackled limbs and souls as freight.

A British minister inspects a cell to which her uncle sent
the rebel colonist who brought his people independence.
She gives a hush-voiced interview as if it were a shrine.

If any governments exist two hundred years from now in countries
still un-flooded and un-fried they'll probably profess
a deep respect for eco-mobs who bravely blocked our roads.

Activists who make the landlord fix
those flaws in his estate he tried to hide
have done his heirs a favour – even those
old Mr Punch-style diehards who believe
the way to do it is to batter down
all upstarts who disturb the status quo.

Cause them to know the abominations of their fathers. **Ezekiel 20:4**

Ezekiel addresses the difficulty of finding fault with one's forbears. Matt 23:29–31
makes a similar point. A shelter commemorating the Tolpuddle Martyrs was
erected in 1934 by London draper Sir Ernest Debenham. Emily Davison's fatal
protest took place at Epsom in June 1913.

ESCAPING. THE CONSEQUENCES

We didn't have to follow them.
It wouldn't take much skin off my nose
if a bunch of slaves who grabbed their kids
and wives and fled the slums around the sweatshops
made it to the coast.
Good for them, I would have said.
If anyone had asked.

It's well beyond a conscript's pay grade
to chase civilians down a beach
when the tide is turning in their favour.
That water holding back beyond their footprints
couldn't last for long.
When luck smiles on the other side
it's rash to push your own.

      But our beloved field commanders knew
      what made the colonels tick back at HQ
      where they had time to learn to read the minds
      of politicians they might like to dine with.
      Thin-skinned ministers don't mix with losers.

So armoured cars were sent in front
to head off trudging refugees
and turn them back toward our waiting weapons.
Fancy vehicles are fine and good
when the going's easy:
gung-ho drivers come unstuck –
then stuck – on soggy sand.

If only we had held our ground
and let the water's surface close
like new- grown skin across the episode,
repairing grievances without a scar.
Instead the wound was sealed
still filthy with our rotting corpses
and would never heal.

I caused them to go out of the land of Egypt, and brought them into the wilderness.
Ezekiel 20:10

The familiar story of Israel's escape from Egypt via the parting of the Red Sea appears in Exodus 14:21–28

THE LEADING ACTOR

wasn't playing to the gallery
so the gallery refused to play
into his hands.
     Distracted
by a lavish backdrop
the author hadn't asked for
and the ornate auditorium
the management insisted on constructing,
the audience admired itself
and hoped posteriors would grace
the cushions in the Royal Box.

He was used to planting clues but knew
he'd need more than a few dropped hints
to get past this crowd's self-inflicted
misdirection.
     What a pity
they had turned against the hero
when he was hunted and betrayed.
But how much worse for them,
to overlook the quiet implication
buried in the second act.

They say of me, 'Isn't he a speaker of parables?' **Ezekiel 20:49**

Ezekiel knows how evasiveness pretends to be unsure what should be taken
literally and what is metaphor.

WHITEWASH

The whitewash would be bad enough –
smeared across that tumbled wall
of crumbling mortar, mildewed stones
and sliding down in clotting dribbles
varicose as old men's veins.

The whitewash would be bad enough
as camouflage without the fiction
it can do repairs. Thick icing
smoothes rough edges but won't mend
that bitter taste of part-burned cake.

The whitewash would be bad enough
but the gap is worse – it is
a forecast of complete collapse
and puts an end to all pretending
whiter whitewash might yet work.

> *Her princes ... are like wolves ravening the prey, to shed blood, and to destroy souls,*
> *that they may get dishonest gain. Her prophets have plastered for them with*
> *whitewash, seeing false visions, and divining lies to them.* **Ezekiel 22:27–28**

I, WILLIAM BLAKE

A boy believes in angels up an oak tree
on the way to Croydon. That's OK:
what's to disbelieve when curtains
cutting off this world from any others
are thin as yellow skeletons of autumn leaves?
Nature's drapes and angel wings
look pretty much the same
and spread or fold as fleetingly
as sparkle-shimmers flash across our eyes
when low sun strikes a window pane.

He looks out now through pity's casement.
Cold wind blows across the common,
scatters morning's opportunities
beyond the reach of any small blue hands
not plunged in hollow pockets
or clasped round chests and tucked in armpits
of a worn-out crumpled jacket, left unwanted,
like its wearer, underneath a hedge.

> *The people of the land have used oppression and exercised robbery. Yes, they have*
> *troubled the poor and needy.* **Ezekiel 22:29**

The poem refers to the 2016 Ken Loach film "I, Daniel Blake" about failings in
the British social security system. As a child, William Blake claimed to have seen
visions on Peckham Rye, including one of "a tree filled with angels, bright angelic
wings bespangling every bough like stars."

PROFILING

All we'll ever have to know.
is this: we wouldn't care to be
like them. So we can't think they care
much for themselves. We shouldn't let
them carry on in parallel
but interact and intervene
to break bad habits they get born to.

Untidy lives aren't soon re-shaped:
a mess disturbed's no less a mess
and therefore we must treat them firmly
till they learn to grasp our rules.
We're not reluctant to be harsh
since years of crude, unschooled survival
must have thickened their resistance –

like their scarred and calloused skin –
to a layer of resilience
which can shrug off any milder
measures weakness might impose.
It would be foolish to assume
that most of them are capable
of feeling pain the way we do.

... and they have oppressed the foreigner wrongfully. **Ezekiel 22:29**

FILLING A VACANCY

The gap is where a man should stand –
while it's still narrow he could touch
both broken sides; and, like a gate,
admit the truth that justified
whatever reckoning was due.

The gap is where a man should stand
who knows the swerve and surge of tides
enough to make a barrier
and save a cache of unspoiled goods
from being swamped or swept away.

The gap is where a man should stand:
but if no local hero comes
the greedy space will ask for more
than human-sized repair – perhaps
a feeding trough, some wooden beams.

> *I sought for a man among them who would build up the wall and stand in the gap*
> *before me for the land, that I would not destroy it; but I found no one.* **Ezekiel 22:30**

MOURNERS

Their first funeral. Two children
won't expect to see their parents,
later, chuckling over scotch
or unaccustomed sweetish sherry.

On the evening of the day
he's seen his father die, a husband
shocks his wife by coming home
in his Dad's old pullover.

A stay-home daughter hears ghost footsteps
in empty bedrooms overhead.
She does and doesn't want the phantom
to descend the actual stairs.

Beside the hearse, a sudden widow,
unprepared for utter change,
counterfeits a smiling face
to soothe an anxious grandchild's fears.

A widower's concealed distress
was less for what was lost than what
he stalked for years and kept pretending
not to know he'd never have.

> *behold, I will take away from you the desire of your eyes with a stroke: yet you shall*
> *neither mourn nor weep, neither shall your tears run down. Sigh, but not aloud.*
> *Make no mourning for the dead.* **Ezekiel 24:16–17**

Ezekiel is told to maintain a public stoicism after the sudden death of his wife in
order to portray the patience with which God had endured the nation's
unfaithfulness.

A SEQUENCE OF EVENTS

I can't forget the way your birthday cake was spoiled.

Did it have to be a *birthday* cake
to plant a fear of disappointing party guests
on top of simple waste and mess?

Of course the birthday cake was only *yours*
because you'd planned and baked and decorated it
the day before as a surprise

and then you boxed it carefully to carry
to the birthday girl a street or two away.
You decided not to take your purse

so you could hold it with both hands – except
for when you'd have to stop and push the crosswalk button.
So perhaps you failed to press it

or the driver missed the light's change, kept on
going, made you jump and drop your sponge . It smashed
to crumbs across the path between

your friend, who hadn't been expecting you
and your poor husband fretting all that afternoon
because you hadn't come home yet.

I can't forget his twelve-hour wait for any news.

So I spoke to the people in the morning; and at evening my wife died. **Ezekiel 24:18**

FALLING BODIES
11 September 2001

Most of us, who heard the witnesses
gasp out their stories or saw photographs
and films we can't forget, will never know

> how many times
> a voice can yell a name or curse
> in five remaining seconds, tumbling
> through the world's accelerating centre

> how fast a heart beats
> when a beast which feeds on speed
> has seized it, sensing freefall's smell
> as sharks detect a spreading smudge of blood

> how wide the eyes go
> seeing downward distance shrink –
> the only certainty to own
> till instinct slams lids shut before the impact

> how hard it is
> to breathe mid-plunge while angled limbs
> tear emptiness to turbulence
> that snatches air away from nose & mouth.

Are these unknowns the worst – the ones appalled, half-willing
watchers have to step away from
treating as real questions that have answers?

To know too much leaves less room on a ledge for hopes
or prayers that sweet angels caught
and stopped their thoughts before they struck the stones.

They will destroy the walls of Tyre, and break down her towers. **Ezekiel 26:4**

TIME AND TALL SHIPS

Suppose a schooner's oaken flanks could stretch
like putty: a continuum of vesselness
riding on a feathered chalk-line wake
whose prow is here and now
while aft it passes through a home port
to a shipyard where it splits
into trajectories of single oaken planks.

An albatross, white-winged and hovering
above the heaving waves, transcends
whatever's measured by their steady tempo.
She can watch each mile and moment
which that hyper-clipper occupies.
She's free to settle anywhere
along the pencil-masthead's trace.

Imagining elastic galleons
as analogues of timelines
makes our past seem so much less
an archipelago of memories
and more a joined-up terra nova:
we arrive where we have never been
and find ourselves still there.

All the ships of the sea with their mariners were in you. **Ezekiel 27:9**

CONNECTING WITH THE WRECK

While Tom's elsewhere, she shops for curios.
One day she finds a wartime postcard of an airship
shot down then washed up on nearby sands.
She sees the tangled girder mess in tattered fabric
as both prophecy and parody
of her shattered, shabby marriage: awkward limbs
at scarecrow angles; two cold souls half-wrapped in bed sheets.

Her heart was never rightly put together.
Leaky valves let hope escape so buoyancy
is lost and she is often overcome
by tight-clenched fears, especially in bed at night.
And is it self-importance or hot air
that keeps his skin so taut? If that were burned away
by shame, his suit would hide a blackened skeleton.

She guesses there were bodies stiff as his discovered
in the airship's wreck. But she identifies
with chilled survivors clinging to a broken structure
drifting with the flotsam till picked up
by enemies. Is capture while escaping
with one's life good luck or bad? She isn't sure
if she'd prefer a prison to a headstone.

She imagines how the empty hulk was tethered,
taken under tow then hauled offshore,
cut free and left to founder. After one brief surge
the placid ocean would have pulled itself together
as if nothing of importance had occurred.
She wishes she could replicate that makeshift mix
of burial at sea and clean annulment.

> *... and all the pilots of the sea will come down from their ships. They will stand on the land, and will cause their voice to be heard* **Ezekiel 27:29–30**

Ezekiel's "pilots of the sea" are here linked to two unrelated facts: (1) on the night of April 5th 1916 Zeppelin L15 was shot down over the Thames estuary and later beached at Margate; (2) T S Eliot and his wife stayed for a while in Margate in 1921.

SPEAK WEALTH

Speak Wealth!
Let this be your language now!
Hold forth on *offshore holdings*;
rhapsodize on *themed investments*;
make a song and dance about
financial instruments.
And don't *short sell* yourself. You're smart
as Archimedes: *leverage*
will lift you up the *rich list*.

Speak Wealth
so we can overhear you.
Boast into your mobile phone
or get the media to tell us
of your newest acquisition,
your most recent self-indulgence.

We get by on smaller change –
the sort that fits in off-peak meters,
slot machines or gaps in floorboards.
We must juggle obligations,
as we walk the fraying wire
stretched between each pair of paydays;
this makes us proficient
in precarious arithmetic.

We perform for pence outside
the court for petty debtors. Elsewhere,
in soft-leather-furnished chambers,
lawyers speak forensic Wealth
to demonstrate non-payment
of your *fiscal liabilities*
is not a fraudulent *evasion*
but permissible *avoidance*.

*

Speak Wealth and you'll be listened to.
Abundance and Authority
both begin with A; and likewise
there's a valid link between
Prosperity and Piety.
Speak Wealth and it can sound like scripture.
After all, the Bible says
To those who have shall more be given
(but we have-nots aren't exempt
from losing even what we have).
We're confident this verse endorses
your strong views on *market forces*.
Oddly though it fails to mention
Trickle Down – that's your invention –
since another scripture states
You'll always have the poor with you.

So if you want to camouflage
this *status* that's routinely *quo*
distract us with the parable
where Dives spares a kindly word
for Lazarus outside his gate:
*Watch out! Some poorer men might come
and try to steal your begging bowl!*

*

Wealth speakers learn unwritten rules
and only talk of *speculating*
in the future perfect tense.
Best not to use the verb *to lose*
unless it's in the past historic.
You'll soften your imperatives
by putting on a passive voice –
*We really are to be believed
but those who doubt us can't be trusted –*
while a subtly placed subjunctive
makes a *no* sound less oppressive:
*It would not be right for us
to increase payments at this time.*

The plural form is much preferred
for third- and second-person pronouns –
not the first though: that's employed
as singular exclusively.

*

Classic dialects of Wealth
abandon too-direct commands
in favour of oblique suggestion.
Simply murmur *It's quite dark*
as if the words could conjure up
a string of instant fairy lights
and a working power source
without a tiresome need to mention
dynamos and armatures
or cables, trenches, spades and sweat.

We cannot match such eloquence
and manage only pidgin forms
of how you talk – which must offend
an ear expecting standard Wealth
the way it's always been received.
So if you're smug and you dismiss
the thought of us acquiring Wealth
even as a second language;
if, with all your fluency
in affluence, you tell yourself
that you can pay whatever price
you put upon your self-esteem…

… you'll have to bear the cost of this:
There's none of us would want to be
mistaken for a native speaker.

> *by your trading you have increased your riches, and your heart is lifted up because of*
> *your riches* **Ezekiel 28:5**

Ezekiel warns the king of Tyre that great wealth brings pride and a sense of
entitlement. The poetic response is modelled on Michèle Lalonde's famous 1974
macaronic poem 'Speak White' which expresses Francophone anger at English-
language dominance in Quebec Province. *youtube.com/watch?v=0hsifsVi2po*

PUT OUT THAT LIGHT!

In the end we've done it for ourselves.
We've said *let there be light* so much it's filled
our night-time streets and now it overflows.
Too late for crying over how it's spilled
as shining mist and masked the Milky Way.

With feeble glows we've picked a silly fight
with vast, far-off, celestial radiances
and won. Our prize is privacy – the right
not to be seen by – and not see – what might be out there.

Divinely offered *lamps unto our feet*
and lights unto our path made some believe
angelic usherettes would come to meet
us stumbling in the dark and sit us down to watch

screened hints on how to overcome life's trials.
We don't want meet-and-greeters any more:
their torches stay switched on along the aisles
so no one in the house can really see the film.

Some learned long ago not to insist
on artificial light and made a truce
with authentic dark. Wide skies exist
in which our forebears learned that counting stars
reminded them of who and where they were.

I will make all the bright lights of the sky dark over you and set darkness on your land
Ezekiel 32:7

"Mankind is proceeding to envelop itself in luminous fog" is a warning from
Italian astronomer Pierantonio Cinzano. "Put out that light!" was supposed to be
the stock command of air raid wardens enforcing blackout during the bombing
of London in World War 2.

CHARISMA OF A FALSE PROPHET

Those who worked with him adored the way
he stroked their keys; but they cared less what tunes he played
on their behalf to woo the public.

His communication skills were highly praised
by those who understood communication skills
were better than communication.
> *Along the wires his scripted sound-bites came*
> *some sharp, some blunter – some, quite frankly, lame.*

And those who owned the bandstands and the bands
that played the nation's marching songs, convinced themselves
the crowds would sing if he conducted.

Some envied his ability to mimic
many voices, from a winning boyish treble
to a trusty baritone.
> *To sound sincere, his bloke-ish accent came*
> *with built-in tremor; and he liked to claim*

he wasn't devious. And that worked well
provided his arrangers had his wheedling tunes
transposed into a major key

and till his stock in trade of skills ran out
of steam and fashion and he failed and kept on failing
to communicate regret.
> *Yet on the screens his well-oiled smile still came*
> *from time to time. It didn't stop the blame.*

you are to them as a very lovely song of one who has a pleasant voice, and can play well on an instrument. **Ezekiel 33:32**

Choruses are variations on a couplet about a royal invalid, attributed to Alfred Austin (Poet Laureate 1896–1913). It runs "Across the wires the electric message came / he is no better, he is much the same"

BUSINESS PLAN

Of course we see them all as wool on legs
then ultimately meat
and only really count them
when they really count –
at times of shearing or slit throats.

What else matters but a flock to market
at the proper time
and with the least expense
to us in risk and blisters?
If some are lost along the way

that still turns out to give us better value
for our cash and sweat
than hiring boys to keep them
together and alive,
by chasing after all the strays.

From a distance, sheep are picturesque
and so are lambs close up:
if you are a consumer
maybe that is all
you know and all you need to know.

Fact is, led or driven, sheep are buggers
to get organised:
that bunch of shiftless drifters,
is still better off
with us than with the local wolves.

> *Shouldn't the shepherds feed the sheep? You haven't healed that which was sick. You haven't bound up that which was broken. You haven't brought back that which was driven away. You haven't sought that which was lost, but you have ruled over them with force and with rigor.* **Ezekiel 34:2–4**

CHORUSES FROM THE FLOCK

As one sheep to another – where do you think we are going?
As one sheep to another – is my anxiety showing?
I can't see see the shepherd or the rest of the flock
so have we got stranded behind this rock?
As one sheep to another – we all should have gone the same way.

As one sheep to another – who do you think you are shoving?
As one sheep to another – please be a little more loving.
But the same goes for me as it does for you:
I've become quite accomplished at pushing too.
As one sheep to another – I'll try not to get in your way.

As one sheep to another – why are you trampling my dinner?
As one sheep to another – can't you see I'm getting thinner?
Yet sheep should be smart enough to understand
we won't go short of grass in the promised land.
As one sheep to another – how much do you reckon you weigh?

As one sheep to another – when did we start all this fighting?
As one sheep to another – that's my bad leg you are biting!
We shouldn't be going for each other's throats:
so let's pause and thank God that we're not goats!
As one sheep to another – can we agree *that* anyway!

> Behold, I judge between sheep and sheep… Does it seem a small thing to you to have
> fed on the good pasture, but you must tread down with your feet the residue of your
> pasture? I will judge between the fat sheep and the lean sheep [b]ecause you thrust
> with side and with shoulder **Ezekiel 34:17–21**

HEART TRANSPLANTS – SIDE EFFECTS & FAQS

Rejection is a major issue
when a doctor takes a stone-still heart
and substitutes donated tissue.

But if physicians have dismissed you
as a hopeless case you'll take the risk –
rejection's not your biggest issue.

At the brink of that abyss you
wish you had been born with nerves of steel
instead of much-too-nervous tissue.

When something inside's gone amiss you
might not need replacement body parts
so much as fresh supplies of *sisu*.

*

You meet your surgeons who address you
only from behind a mask: perhaps
because they do not want to face you?

You're told by the anaesthetist you
sleep before you've counted down from ten.
You hope his needle doesn't miss you.

You dream that nurses come and kiss you
wearing scrubs – are antiseptic pecks
distractions so they can undress you?

And when you start to convalesce, you
don't get solid food: will you survive
digesting only tiramisu?

*

I'll turn your stone hearts into flesh: you   ...
needn't care what rocks you'll lose – your faith
in miracles is what's at issue.

If old resentment finds a fissure
in your new-made heart my remedy
is grafting in forgiving tissue.
(Redemption is a bigger issue.)

> *I will also give you a new heart, and I will put a new spirit within you. I will take*
> *away the stony heart out of your flesh, and I will give you a heart of flesh.*
> **Ezekiel 36:26**

Sisu is a Finnish word whose meaning can be approximated by a combination of
such concepts as stoicism and determined resistance.

DEM BONES

This is has gone beyond embarrassing.
Speeded-up perceptions find
they have the time to comment on
a white van slo-mo overcoming
pedestrian resistance.

Right leg triple open fracture.
It's wiser not to look at blood
or bone so opt for a distraction ...
make adrenaline-induced apologies
to anyone who comes to help.

I think we put the bits all back.
A shattered tibial plateau
can be repaired: a wire mesh matrix
holds the crumbled mess in place
supported on titanium.

It only needs a blood supply
to grow itself as good as new.
The mended bone will end up stronger
than its metal reinforcement
which gets weakened by fatigue.

Keep this card. It states what kind
of orthopaedic screw we used.
A surgeon can imagine nothing worse
than opening a patient up
then finding half your tools won't fit.

Then the bones came together, bone to its bone. **Ezekiel 37: 7**

The poem title refers to a 1928 song by James Weldon Johnson based on
Ezekiel 37.

A LACK OF LIMINALITY

Occupants of private dovecotes
are cooing by appointment
to the present owners of the Manor,
echoing wild pigeons crooning
in his Lordship's arboretum.

Meanwhile scores of us are queuing
for the garden Open Day.
Grass tempts some of us to sprawl,
as if we're sun-warmed six-year-olds.

The guide book, like an eager salesman,
urges us to choose between
two paths of brick, like fallen walls,
taking us toward The Maze –
a puzzle with a known solution –
or The Wilderness, a self-
directed course in getting lost.

Alas, a designated wasteland
on a flimsy Xeroxed plan
lacks the *frisson* of a caption
here be dragons scrawled on parchment.

But here at least there do be dragon-
flies above the lily-pond
where water boatmen scuttle round
bewildered bigger insects trapped
in surface tension till they drown.

The water rather than the air
creates a thin protective skin
which – like this garden's long brick wall –
knows whose it is and knows its job's
to keep the inside undisturbed.

Think of any interface
of *this* with *that* and ask which side
solidifies its border first?
Who protests? Who will comply?
How many simply slip across?
Does who transcends and who transgresses
vary with which way they're going?
What if contraband's involved?

Distinctions between *one* and *other*
may not offer room for *both*.
So butterflies which come too close
to where they don't and can't belong
will die because they brush against
a surface that says *either/or*.

We're told we ought to know our place
as land or sea and name our time
as day or night. But you can't map
a coastline made of sand-grain fractals;
dark and light give ground to dusk.

Not all boundaries are thin
as shadows thrown against a wall:
moist means *neither* drenched *nor* parched;
and threading of a maze depends
on sharp turns left *as well as* right.
What a shame we find it hard
to see we're free to slide *between*
the hoi polloi *and* le beau monde.

There was a wall between me and them **Ezekiel 43:8**

Whatever walls may or may not exist between the human and the divine there are
plenty which have been constructed between human and human.

SOCIAL DISTANCING

We are managing the situation.

Whenever people flow like water
through the holy interlocking boxes
of a stadium, emporium
or auditorium, their leaders
and role models must be seen among them
only briefly rubbing elbows –
never pressing hands – and passing on
no more than they brought in with them.
They are all in this together.

As they stream through lobbies,
passages and concourses
from north and south not one of them
may leave the way they entered.
All turnstile counters click in one direction
for the regular attenders;
any strangers, misfits
or occasional creatives
have to slip through gaps in calculation.

> *he who enters by the way of the north gate to worship shall go out by the way of the*
> *south gate; and he who enters by the way of the south gate shall go out by the way of*
> *the north gate. He shall not return by the way of the gate by which he came in, but*
> *shall go out straight before him.* **Ezekiel 46:9,10**

It seems almost as if Ezekiel foresaw Covid restrictions!

INCARNATION

You burst into our conversation
like the sudden stranger
striding through a bar room.
You split our boasting, wooing, whining
with a silence measured
by the rolling tick-tock
of a toppled empty glass;
the drop of dominoes
dribbling off a table;
the ripple of a pack of cards
self-shuffling while escaping
from a dealer's grip.

Before the raising of a voice
you cut the moment short
and quit the floor, to let
the laughter and the bartering
choose to start again.
The swing doors spread and shut
behind your unprotected back
as if to beckon any
who might dare to follow,
empty-handed and alone,
and face you in the dark
beyond the disused stable.

When the prince enters, he shall go in by the way of the porch of the gate, and he shall go out by its way. **Ezekiel 46:8**

MIGRANTS

To go up in the world choose London places –
Hoxton, Stepney, Bow ... And Islington
at night is fascinating – it's like Heaven!

Water flowing eastward from a city
meets resistance, spreads out wide to wash
the buried, unremembered dead, abandoned
by a banished people, wandering and weeping
for the future of their born and unborn children

Always on the radio there's politics,
and politics and politics. What is this politics
that means I have to leave my Mum & Dad?

This side chasing that side. Our side shooting their side.
Children don't have ways of dealing with that stuff.
I still remember mother thinking cushions
in the window ought to stop the bullets.

This river must entice each family
into its shallows, draw them ankle-deep
downstream away from where the rough and tumble,
flotsam-tossing torrent won't distinguish toddlers
in a crush of pilgrims, fugitives or logs.

There was watermelon that last night
but nobody explained. I never said goodbye.

It felt like being dragged along by water.
No one asked me – Do you want to leave?

Even a child of seven knew there were too many
crammed in our small boat on that big ocean.
You could touch the water with your hand.

I didn't have an accent till they laughed at it;
then told me there was more than one religion.

Deeper water pacifies the backwash
from a toxic ocean. Currents join
in brackish discourse to negotiate
safe passage through the estuary where swimmers rest
at last, afloat on joy and cradling hopes like babies…

> *Hackney's everything – everything is Hackney!*
> *Sometimes I sit in Stratford International*
> *pretending I am going back to where I started.*
> *But when I try to dream of being somewhere else*
> *it's always Stepney that remains my proper home.*

*These waters flow out … toward the sea; and flow into the sea … and the waters will
be healed.*
*[Y]ou shall divide [the land] by lot for an inheritance to you and to the aliens who
live among you, who will father children among you. Then they shall be to you as the
native-born* **Ezekiel 47: 8 & 22**

This partly-found poem is adapted from voices heard in Eithne Nightingale's film
Child Migrant Stories, childmigrantstories.com

REVISING THE VISION

Editors need good intentions when they proof-read
prophecy; so on Page One they only mean
to fix the grammar without overbalancing
a golden ratio of dreams to dogma.

But it's hard for them to curb their urge to drop
big blocks of orthodoxy on the seer's pool
of bright quicksilver speculation till it splits
to shining pellets scuttling in the dust.

So they've blue-pencilled in an extra character.
That urban runner's back again, still bronzed and fit
but slower now; and he has had enough of pounding
on and on through steep and narrow streets.

They've sent him in to prowl the prose like a surveyor
measuring the breadth of ambiguities
and setting bounds on supposition. They can't let
illicit schemes slip through to get approved.

These editors read documents like city plans:
sentences are one-way streets; and arguments
are bridges that won't flex beneath their footsteps. Statics
trumps dynamics for the pious draughtsmen.

Once a rule's been laid across a prophecy
its mystery is fixed. No scope for shape-shifts. Straight-faced,
straight-edged editors can't help strait-jacketing
the splendid lunacies of holy fools.

*behold, there was a man, whose appearance was like the appearance of bronze, with a
line of flax in his hand, and a measuring reed; and he stood in the gate.* **Ezekiel 40:3**

It is believed that the Book of Ezekiel was compiled and edited by several hands.
The careful descriptions of a rebuilt city in later chapters lack the vivid
imagination shown in earlier sections. Perhaps a number of these editors – like
some present-day readers – were uneasy about Ezekiel's visionary outspokenness.